In My Words

In My Words

Stories of an Autistic Boy

Written and Illustrated by

Robbie Clark

Inserts from Rob Clark, Maggie Clark and Emma Clark

Library of Congress Control Number: 2016907016
ISBN: Hardcover   978-1-5144-8980-2
               Softcover   978-1-5144-8979-6
               eBook   978-1-5144-8978-9

Print information available on the last page.

Rev. date: 05/03/2016

To order additional copies of this book, contact:
Xlibris
1-888-795-4274
www.Xlibris.com
Orders@Xlibris.com
738600

Foreword

If you had told me twenty-two years ago I would be writing a foreword for my son's book about his life dealing with autism, I would have never believed you. Twenty-two years have passed, and here we are, doing just that thing.

Nothing prepares you for the day when you find out your child is not what many people would describe as typical. I remember very clearly the day we found out our son was diagnosed as a child with autism. I had one of those life-flashing experiences where everything you dreamed about is about to be thrown for an unimaginable loop. When you become a parent, you have this vision of wanting the perfect family—coaching T-ball, seeing him leave for prom, taking him to college, and one day, getting married and having a family himself. That vision was crushed by a one-page letter telling us our son was autistic.

A child with special needs changes everyone and everything around them. There were years of doctors and tests, years of therapy of all kinds, and years of meetings with schoolteachers and principals that none of us were prepared for. Learning to balance our time within our family with our daughter to make sure she felt just as important yet make her understand some things have to be different for the sake of being different.

Writing this and looking back all these years brings back the whole gambit of emotions our family experienced. Robbie writing this book is just a small example of how Robbie continues to make a huge impact on the lives of the people he has come in contact with. The smallest things you and I take for granted have been large victories in our family.

This book describes many situations Robbie and our family has dealt with over the years. As you read, you may find grammatical errors, but we felt it was important for Robbie's thoughts to come out. And although we all could improve our grammar, we thought it would help you understand more of his story. Some experiences Robbie writes about are funny, while some speak to the always-too-frequent not-so-funny experiences. This gives the reader a chance to get a perspective from all points of view in certain situations. I hope this book is a great insight for people to learn more about special-needs people and how just a small token or gesture makes a world of difference in the eyes of a family or person with special needs, hopefully for the better, and in this case, it couldn't be more the truth.

I don't know how he does it, but he is like a leader on a sports team. He makes everyone around him a better person. He makes you want to work harder, play harder, and enjoy the simple things in life. He is quiet at first meet, but his sense of humor is sneaky good, and don't let him fool you—he knows what's going on.

Robbie is special but in the best kind of way. He has made everyone around him a better person and continues to make an enormous impact on the lives of people around him. I think when it comes down to it, all parents want to be proud of their children. We have two wonderful children, whom we couldn't be more proud of. He is proof that with effort and lots of love, special-needs people can become normal in most every sense of the word. That's all Robbie has ever wanted to be, and that's all we have ever wanted for Robbie.

Rob Clark

Preface

When I was young kid, I found it hard to express my emotions. I had no idea I was a child with special needs. I learned emotions from drawing them on a piece paper so I could communicate with my family and friends. Today we call these drawings emojis. I decided to write this book to help explain how some people with autism have trouble explaining their feelings.

I also wanted to take this opportunity to thank the many people who helped me through the years: the teachers, therapists, friends, and family. There are too many to mention, but know that my family and I think of all of you all the time. It is all these people who gave me inspiration to write this book. Thank you to all people who provided help and support for my book, especially Mrs. Jackie Reeves and my teacher and friend Erin Sullivan.

Lastly, I want to thank my family for all their support and understanding. There is no substitute for a loving and caring family. I especially want to thank my mom for always believing in me. She never gives up on me and pushes me to always do the right thing and my best.

I hope you enjoy my book.

All about Me: Robbie

My name is Robbie Clark, and I am a twenty-two-year-old boy who lives in Huntsville, Alabama. I'm just like most kids; I like LSU sports, watching movies, drawing, painting, and just hanging out. The one thing that might make me a little different than most twenty-two-year-olds is that I have autism. To me, autism means a disorder. When asked by my dad if I knew what that meant, I said, "Yes, it means not in order."

I was born in Baton Rouge, Louisiana, in 1993. I was the proud child of Maggie and Rob Clark. I was so eager to come into this world. The doctors had to prevent me from coming early at twenty-eight weeks. In week 32, I couldn't take it any longer and was happy to meet the world. My first year was just like most babies' first year, learning to sit up, crawl, and then eventually, to walk. Although there were concerns about my delayed development within my family, our pediatrician assured us all was good and it is not uncommon for a premature baby to be delayed. As you read further through the book, you will get perspectives from all sides of the family. You will hear from my mom and dad as well as my sister.

My hope for this book is to give encouragement to others like me and to their families who are beginning this journey. I also hope it will give other family members some insight on the struggles and victories of my journey. Most importantly, I want people to realize, sometimes, it can be the simplest things that can make a difference in someone's life. Sometimes, these acts may have a lasting negative effect, while others can give someone a warm feeling of love. Many times, it is easy to ignore emotions of people with autism because they have a hard time expressing themselves. I can assure you we go through all the emotions of being scared, happy, sad, hurt, excited, and more. Hopefully, this book will help show that.

When I Knew: Mom

When Robbie was about three years old, Emma, his little sister, was just an infant. We were at our home in Baton Rouge. I was busy feeding Emma and asked Robbie to put his *A*, *B*, and *C* foam letters in order for me. He started grabbing a letter at a time and placing them on the floor. All the letters were pushed in a pile and completely out of order. Robbie began grabbing letters off the top of the pile randomly.

I watched in amazement as he carefully placed letters in precise position in three rows. He picked up the *L*, placing it on the second row, then an *R*, etc. He placed every letter with no hesitation. I was sitting there, having to count back in my head the *H*, *I*, *J*, *K* to know what went in which position. There was a toddler with very little understandable verbal communication, and he was laying out the alphabet in order with ease. My thoughts after the shock was, *He's so smart. He's a bright little boy. Now, what else does he know?*

First Memories: Dad

Besides the memories of spending time with my son in the hospital when he was born, I think the first real memory I have about Robbie is when we read the letter from a doctor in Dallas, which read, "Robbie shows characteristics of Autism." Let me preface this with I'm terrible with exact dates and I'm envious of people who can call out a year and talk specifically about the events and the order of which they happened. Anyway, I clearly remember sitting in my bedroom with my wife and her parents, reading the letter stating our son had autism. My very first thought was the movie *Rain Man*. That was my only knowledge of autism at that point. I remember my head spinning with thoughts of *Will my son play baseball? Will he go to school? Will he get married and have children? Will he live on his own?* Looking back, it is hard to imagine at the time that I would make it through all that, but somehow, I just did.

Talking Is Tough Sometimes: Robbie

When I talk, I understand that some people have a hard time hearing what I have to say. Or they simply aren't listening and put too much thought into what I say. This makes me so mad and frustrates me. People ask me the same questions over and over again. They don't hear me or misinterpret what I have to say. I am not meaning to be rude, as I know that is not nice. I know I have been rude to people before, but I didn't mean to.

I try really hard to fit in with everyone. I make sure to always listen to others when they talk to me and not to interrupt them when they are talking. I like to give my friends and family hugs when I see them 'cause I love them. I always listen to my friends and have always just wanted to be like them. I make an effort to speak as clearly as possible and slow down when I talk so it will make it easier for everyone to understand me. Sometimes, I just get so excited about what I have to say that I get rushed.

I usually talk more around people I know well. I also talk to anyone about Disney and/or award shows as I know a lot about them. Just because I don't talk a lot doesn't mean that I don't have a lot to say or don't know a lot. I actually am pretty smart.

A Day in Wal-Mart: Mom

Another day I remember very clearly is a day that Robbie and I headed to Wal-Mart to do our weekly shopping. Robbie was just two years old, and I was quite pregnant with Emma. Anyway, our routine was, we would arrive at Wal-Mart and stop into the McDonald's located at the front entrance of the store. We would get an order of fries and a drink and head out to get our groceries. However, on this given day, one of their fryers was down, and thus, it was taking two to three minutes for them to push out orders of fries. Well, many of you might not think much of these two to three minutes, but Robbie proceeded to scream at the top of his lungs for the full two to three minutes. Oh, the looks we were given.

Now, most people could have just tried to explain, "Hey, it's just going to take a couple minutes. Let's look at this Disney magazine" or "I know it's going to take a couple minutes. If you are good while we wait, I will buy you a toy." And of course, I am sure that was what was going through all those shoppers' minds that morning. However, they didn't understand. Robbie could not be bribed. He didn't understand the concept of "If I do this, I can get that." Most parents don't appreciate this simple task: "If you are good, we will get . . ." We had to teach Robbie this concept through a program called ABA (Applied Behavior Analysis). So all Robbie knew on that given day in Wal-Mart was, "I'm not getting my fries that I always get when we come. What have I done wrong?"

Keep this story in mind. Next time you come across an uncontrollable screaming kid. Maybe there's more to the story.

Perspective: Dad

Early on, when you have been told your child is autistic, it kind of sets you back a little. Eventually, you come out of the funk, and that's when you begin to learn special things. One could look at our lives and feel pity on us for all we have had to go through. That is one way to look at it. However, I would like to share a different perspective. How many times in our lives did our parents tell us we needed to get our priorities straight? I'm here to tell you, having a child with autism will put your priorities in perspective. Little victories mean the world to everyone involved.

One in particular is back when Robbie was five years old. We were driving in my truck, and at the time, I had really never heard more than "One, two, three, weeeeee!" There were times when I felt Robbie was never going to talk where I could understand him. He would grunt, motion, or ramble on as to be having a full conversation without a single word being understandable.

Anyway, one day, we were driving down the interstate, and I was talking to my mother on the cell phone. As we approached an overpass, there was the McDonald's golden arches way up in the sky. The first words I had ever heard come from my son's mouth was "I want to go to McDonald's." Clear as anything, one complete, full sentence just like that! I just about lost control of the truck. I had been around this child for five years, and nothing had come out of his mouth that could be the least bit discernible.

I looked back in the rearview mirror and asked him, "What?" He repeated, "I want to go to McDonald's." Needless to say, I hung up on my mom with her still talking and drove straight to McDonald's, where I think we ate twice. It was small little victories like this that made our family really sit back and see what is important in life and put things in perspective.

The Beach: Robbie

I don't remember a whole lot about my first trip to the beach with my cousins Kyle and Mike. I was only three or four years old. I do remember everyone talking about how I wouldn't step in the sand. I do know that I didn't like the feel of different things on my hands or feet. Things such as paint, mud, sand, etc., made me feel very uncomfortable and gave me an itchy feeling. Everyone did talk about how much I loved the ocean. I would run into the waves, and they would knock me down, but I would just get up laughing. The feeling of the pounding on my body, I don't know why, but I loved this feeling, and still do today.

However, the next day, I couldn't go into the ocean at all as I would scream when the waves would hit me. But I did sit and walk in the sand on this day. I wouldn't play in it but was okay with getting it on me. Why? I can't explain, just like so many other things in my life. I know that I do some things differently, and people always want to know why, but I can't always explain them.

I do know today, I don't mind the beach at all. In fact, we go about once a year. I do still love the ocean and being in the waves, but I do not like the saltwater in my eyes. It burns them, so I have to get out and wipe them off whenever that happens. I don't mind the sand but don't care to play in it or build a sand castle. I usually get in the ocean, ride waves, or throw a ball with my dad. Or I will sit in a chair under an umbrella because I don't like getting sunburn. Getting sunburn hurts.

I do remember taking trips to the beach and Becky getting to go with us. Becky was our babysitter. Once again, I was little when she would watch us, but I do remember how nice she was. She would take us places and play with us. And now, she is married and has her own kids and talks to me on Facebook all the time. I miss her but always know she loves me.

Kyle, Mike, and Robbie: Robbie

As far back as I can remember, it was always Kyle, Mike, me, and of course, Emma. I do remember at our old house in Baton Rouge, Kyle and Mike would come over all the time. Sometimes we would just watch movies, sometimes we would play with my trains, and sometimes we would go outside and play. I didn't always keep up with them or like doing the things they liked, but they always stayed with me.

With the move from Baton Rouge, it was hard to leave Meme, Papaw, and Grandma, but I really missed Kyle and Mike the most. I always got to go to their house, and they would come stay with me. I love them so much. I loved it when they visited. We still go to the beach with them and have also gone rafting and to the lake with them. I remember going rafting. All the boys got in one raft, and Mom, Emma, and Aunt Kat got in another one. This trip was so much fun and funny. We also went to the lake with them, where we went tubing. I don't know how I stayed on that tube. It had to be 'cause Kyle held on to me.

I am still waiting to go to Disney World with them. I wish I could have gone to school with them; I would have always been okay and even maybe had Mike in some of my classes. All my friends could have met them, and everyone would have known they were my cousins. I would have never been lonely. I miss it being Kyle, Mike, and Robbie.

Stop!: Mom

Every toddler has its way of a temper tantrum. However, this was different. When Robbie would get frustrated, he would throw his head back. This started about twelve months old. He was sitting up on the floor, and I don't even remember what set him off, but he just threw his head back on the floor. We were lucky this time it was on carpet, but that was not always the case. It had to hurt, but it was his way of showing extreme frustration.

Now looking back on it, I can't even imagine wanting to say something so bad—to tell my mom or dad what I wanted or what was hurting me or what I needed—but not knowing how. Therefore, this was something Robbie continued to do till he was about four years old. This behavior landed us in the emergency room, head full of stitches and many knots. As a mom, it was hard. There were many times when I simply felt like I was a failure. What in the world was I doing to have my son do this? I just wanted to protect him but had no idea of what to do other than to just hold him tight and pray. Robbie is almost twenty-three years old, and I still hug him tight and pray.

> Dear Lord, I can't do this alone. I need your help, and I need your guidance. Please protect my child. I have so many fears that he will be taken advantage of and hurt. I want him to soar in your name and know your love. Please guide me each day on how to be a good parent. Amen.

Nowhere to Turn: Mom

Everyone has dreams and hopes of their child attending the perfect school. Rob and I had been blessed with the opportunity to move back to Baton Rouge right before the birth of Robbie. We were getting to go home. Before Robbie was even born, I had gone by St. Luke's Episcopal School to put "Baby Clark" on the waiting list for preschool. This was how competitive it was getting into private schools in the Baton Rouge area. However, this was not just any private school but the school in which I had attended for a few years and the school/church that I had only attended since I was born. This was where Rob and I were married and where Robbie and Emma were baptized, and it would be our home, our church, and the school for our children.

Time had passed. Robbie was diagnosed with autism-like symptoms and had been in and out of therapy since he was two and a half years old. When it came time for Robbie to go to St. Luke's, it was an important time in his life. It was recommended to keep him in as much of a normal setting as possible. It was good for him to have regular peer role modeling. So we were so thankful for our church to have this school available for us, and for Robbie, it was a blessing.

That was until we received a letter from the school, informing us that Robbie would not be accepted into the program. They did have room for Emma in the three-year-old program, but Robbie would not be accepted into the four-year-old program.

You can only imagine the emotions that overwhelmed me. They didn't even call; they just sent a standardized letter. I made an appointment to meet with the school principal and rector, asking for help. I was told the school was sorry, but they were not interested in working with us. I offered to provide a student shadow for him to keep from any disruption of the class. Once again, the church did not want to get involved. The school had too many other students on a waiting list to get in that were considered normal.

Robbie would not attend the school. I felt as if I was just punched in the stomach. Where were we going to go? Robbie needed to be in a preschool setting, where he would role-model off regular students and be pushed to move out of his comfort zone. For the past two years, we had been working with Robbie on the program ABA (Applied Behavior Analysis) and had Robbie be placed in a special therapy program at the Baton Rouge Speech and Hearing Foundation, all to get him ready and prepared to integrate into a regular program.

Now what were we suppose to do? We tried turning to our church, which closed the door on us. Where were we to go? I can honestly say with the way my church had turned a blind eye to us, I couldn't help but have my faith shaken. I can say that even still today, I have a very hard time passing this church on the road, much less having to walk onto its campus. Rob and I left my lifelong church that day, and it wasn't until several years later that we even thought of finding another church to attend.

Teachers Make a Difference: Robbie

I would not be where I am today if so many people would not have stood up for me, fought for me, and spoke up for me. There are so many of you that I can't begin to name you all. However, there is one: Mrs. Fox. Mrs. Fox was my first schoolteacher. I was placed in a noncategory class, which meant that all the kids in my class have some kind of issue. The plan my parents had was that after a year in this class, I would be able to go straight into kindergarten. Mrs. Fox was so nice, and even though I don't remember much of this class, everyone tells me I was really good in it and did really well.

But the school was not convinced that I was ready for a regular kindergarten class. So I had to go into the self-contained autistic class. You will hear stories of how well this went. And then there was Mrs. Fox. Because she was willing to stand up for me, I got the opportunity to be placed in a regular first-grade classroom. Mrs. Fox was willing to do the extra work with Mrs. Anderson, my first grade teacher, and work with her so I could succeed. Mrs. Anderson was willing to take me as a student in her class. She gave me a special seat right by her desk.

I loved being part of this class and having a chance to be like all the other kids. But there were some kids in this class that were so bad. They just would not listen and do what Mrs. Anderson would tell us to do, like talk when she would say "No talking." But we did it, and I successfully completed and passed first grade in the East Baton Rouge School System with good grades. To this day, I believe I was the very first autistic child to be mainstreamed successfully. Thank you, Mrs. Fox, for believing in me.

Contained: Robbie

At Westminster Elementary School, I was in an autistic class. This was a class that had only three kids and me with autism in it, with one teacher and one helper. I did have a regular kindergarten teacher whose class I was supposed to go into so I could be around other kids that didn't have autism. I didn't like being in the autistic class. One of the boys in the class was actually nice to me and became my friend. Another one of the boys would always scream, which would hurt my ears. And there was a boy that would push and bite me. I did not like this class at all. There was always so much yelling and arguing from the kids, the teachers, everyone.

The boys wouldn't sit still and listen to the teacher, and there was always so much going on. I would try and tell them all I was feeling, but they always had trouble understanding me. This would only make me more frustrated. And when I was in the regular class, I would try my best to be right and do as I was told. But it was hard. There was always so much going on, and a lot of times, I just didn't understand what they wanted me to do. So I would not interrupt and try to just be quiet and not misbehave. I was so glad when this year was over and I didn't have to go to that small class anymore. I just wanted to be with all the other kids and be like them.

Bite Marks: Mom

I know we are not the only parents to have a child come home with bite marks from another kid. I still remember it as if it was yesterday. Robbie was in kindergarten and was in a self-contained autistic class that was supposed to be integrated 50 percent of the day. I will let you know the 50 percent of his day they chose to integrate him was recess, PE, and lunch, leaving only a thirty-minute opening for classroom time. They did their 50 percent that was required; our mistake was not designating exactly how this 50 percent should have been assigned.

So Robbie hopped off the bus and ran to give me a hug and had big tears in his eyes. After asking him what was wrong, he held up his arm, where the bite mark was so clear and deep that I could count all upper and lower teeth marks. I was so upset and asked Robbie what happened. All he could say was a classmate's name. I asked what his teacher did, and he didn't say anything. As any parent, I didn't sleep a wink that night and had quite a time even getting Robbie to return to school the next day.

When we made it to school and to his classroom, I asked his teacher and her aid if they had any idea what happened. I showed them Robbie's arm that, by the next day, was swollen and red. Neither one of them was even aware that Robbie had been bitten. There were only four students in this class, with a teacher and an aid. I was floored and, at that point, knew without a doubt this was not the place for Robbie.

What was I going to do? After visiting dozens of private schools, no one was willing to accept him into their regular programs, not even our church. Yes, I could have pulled him out and homeschooled him, but the one thing he needed most was normal peer modeling, and that I could not give him at home, nor was he getting it in his contained classroom. I was not going to give up. This was when we knew that Robbie had to be mainstreamed, and so the fight was on: an IEP meeting, visits to classrooms, and then Mrs. Fox.

Mrs. Fox was Robbie's preschool noncategory teacher, who had since moved into the role of resource teacher. She spoke up and agreed with us that Robbie, with her help, could do it. Robbie did not have a behavior problem; he knew to follow directions, thanks to a program called Applied Behavior Analysis. However, he would need help from resource and us at home to reinforce the assignments. All we knew was, whatever it took, we were in 110 percent!

Family Friends: Robbie

Ben Dupont—I have been told that he was a kid that my dad always looked after. When Ben was growing up, he would hang out at the golf club my dad worked at. So by the time I was born, Ben had been around a lot. One of my first memories of Ben was at our house in Baton Rouge. Ben would always be hanging around the house. Emma says some of her first memories of Mr. Ben were of him sleeping in my bed. He always liked my room because it was the coolest and darkest in the house for him to sleep. I love seeing him when he comes in town. He is so funny and tells lots of jokes. I know just how much he loves me. I'm not sure exactly how or when he became part of the family. All I know is it was before I was born.

In fact, there are lots of people that have come into our family over the years. At one point, Lori was one of those, and Becky, who was our babysitter when we were little. Laura, whom we met here in Huntsville— we love her—and Sam. There was also Joey, who actually lived with us for a while, but we don't get to see him much and miss him. And then all the boys from the club, Anthony, Steven, and Jordan, were with us for a summer. We now have Brad, who spends lots of time with the family. I love all of them and am glad that they spent so much time with us.

It's fun when there is always someone over. When I was little, Emma always had friends over, and that was fun. I could always play with her and her friends if I wanted. Cassidy was like part of the family for a long time. I miss Cassidy; she is so sweet. And Crystal would stay with us a lot.

But Ben was the first. He's my brother now. I know Ben loves me as much as I love him.

The Difficult Side: Emma

When I was asked to write some stories for the book, I was really excited to share my love and life about Robbie. Unfortunately, not everything has been all smiles. There were and are hard times, and it is hard for me to talk about them. When Robbie and I were in elementary school and some of middle school, we did not get along a lot of the time. One, I was a know-it-all little girl who did whatever she wanted. Two, Robbie's temper when we were younger was set off more easily than now. So add those two together, and you have a lot of fighting.

Most siblings fight growing up; that is not uncommon. Robbie used to be rough when he would get overwhelmed or angry. He would hit and scratch. It always scared me. I knew he would never hurt me to where I would be injured, but I knew he would hit me or he would scratch me. Again, this isn't uncommon for siblings. The older I got, the stronger I got, the less scared I got. That was when I started trying to calm him down, making him realize it was okay when he got mad. I started being more like a parent in a way, always trying to talk Robbie through it so he wouldn't get mad. Robbie would get set off by some of the simplest things, and it would bother me a lot because we all had to pay attention to Robbie and basically do what would be best to suit the problem and calm him down.

My parents, by no means, just did whatever Robbie wanted. They would make him learn to get through the situation. It was not just challenging for Robbie but it was also challenging for the rest of the family. Sometimes it would make us uncomfortable and really test our patience. I think this has been a constant reminder in my life today: don't run from your problems; face them straight on.

Starting the Village: Robbie

When I was little, Mom and Dad would have a girl come to the house to help me learn. Her name was Lori; she was my teacher's helper at the Baton Rouge Speech and Hearing Foundation, where I went to preschool when I was little. She was always really nice to me and helped me whenever I needed it. Mom and Dad would also have another girl, named Rebecca, that would come to the house to work with me on my numbers, letters, sentences, and fun things. Lori and Rebecca would also come and babysit Emma and me if Mom and Dad had to go somewhere. They also took us to the park and to play in the ball pits at McDonald's. I never really realized just how much they helped me. Mom and Dad said that Lori and Rebecca's help while I was so young was an important part of why I was able to graduate from high school and actually be able to go to school with Emma and other kids that are not autistic, like me. I don't remember much of it, but I was part of Lori's wedding, where she let me wear a Mickey Mouse bow tie.

I know Lori and Rebecca really love me. I was excited when I got to see Lori at an LSU game a couple of years ago. It had been years since I got to see her. Last time I saw her, she came to see us in Huntsville when she had some work. But this time, she couldn't believe how tall I was. Mom and Dad tell me that Lori and Rebecca will always have a special place in our family. We will always love them.

I Do Understand: Robbie

I know that a lot of the time, people may have a hard time understanding me and don't think that I understand them. But I really do understand them. I understood when I was told to be quiet and to not talk by my teachers. I understand when I am asked to put Hayley Henderson's golf bag on a cart and pull it around for her. I understand all these. Times when I get confused are when they ask me to do too many things all at once. Or when I am asked to do something I have never done before, like driving. I get scared and don't want to do it. What if I mess up? What if I do things wrong? I've never done this before, so I don't know if I can do it right.

I get everyone's feelings. I can sense when someone is upset. I will give them a hug and try to help cheer them up and help them feel better. Just as me, I have feelings too. I get upset, mad, and sad over things as well. I don't want people to be mad or upset with me, so I try and do my best to be nice and love everyone.

Little Things: Robbie

Every summer before school would start, Mom and I would go by my school. Mom had talked to the principal or guidance counselors to make sure they were able to get my class schedule early so I would know what teachers I had. We would go by when they had my schedule ready, and we would walk the halls and find my classes. I would also sometimes run into my new teachers so I could meet them and they would know who I was.

By going by the school early, this really helped me, especially when I got into middle school and high school and there would be lots of different classes I would have to go to. When school started and there would be all the kids in the halls and all the noise, it helped to know where I was going. There were a couple of times when I would get confused and, sometimes, my friends would let me follow them to my next class, or if I just got really confused, then I would just go to my guidance counselor, where I could stay till I knew where to go and was comfortable.

My freshman year at Grissom High School, I would have a new locker. During orientation, it was really hard to get my combination for my locker to work. In middle school, I had my own lock, which I was able to practice at home with. Here at Grissom, the locks were built into the lockers, so I couldn't take it home to practice. Once everyone got their lockers, we were all practicing opening them. I was having a hard time getting mine to open. The more I tried and couldn't get it, the more frustrated I got. My friend Adam Smith stayed with me and helped me even though all his friends were leaving. He stayed and helped me. I thank him for helping me. With his help, I got it.

Comforting Things: Robbie

Mrs. Anderson, my first-grade teacher, would test my temper. I had always carried around at least one or two toys that made me feel comfortable. It was like whenever things were hard, I could look down at these and feel comfortable. At one point, it was my Winnie the Pooh and Tigger figurines, but at this given time, it was my favorite, my Bugs Bunny and Daffy Duck Beanie Babies. I would take these with me to and from school every day. Then one day, I don't remember exactly why, but Mrs. Anderson felt they were interfering with the class and my work. I didn't want to put them away as they were my comfort item. These Beanie Babies went with me everywhere. I would hold on to them while eating, writing, watching TV, everything.

So when Mrs. Anderson took them from me and put them on her desk, this made me so mad. And when it was time to line up for the bus and go home, she still would not let me have them. This was when I lost it. I was not getting on that bus and not going home without my Bugs and Daffy. They called my mom to come get me as I had missed the bus. When my mom got there, she knew just how much these Beanie Babies meant to me and tried to explain to the teachers just how much this was going to upset me all night long. But my mom told me that we would have to leave them there for the night and I would get them back tomorrow. As my parents still remind me, it was indeed a long night. That next morning, I couldn't wait to get to school. As soon as I got to class, I got my Bugs and Daffy and put them in my bag. They never returned to school with me again.

I have since moved on to keeping a pencil in my hand as my comfort item. It doesn't seem to bother people as much.

Not Everyone Gets Me: Robbie

In Baton Rouge, when I was in second grade, my teacher had us working on compound words. We were all to stand in groups. She would have us say certain words and clap while saying them at the same time (for example, *cupcake*, *sidewalk*, etc.). The classroom was getting really loud. Everyone was screaming, clapping, and jumping up and down. I couldn't handle this. Kids were brushing up against me, clapping, and yelling. It was hurting my ears, my eyes were burning, and the feeling of other kids brushing against me felt like needles. Trying to process what I was hearing, seeing, and feeling while trying to clap and talk myself—no way.

I tried to communicate to Mrs. Bell that I could not do this. She just thought I was being bad and couldn't understand. After a few more minutes of this, I didn't know how to make her understand. So I got a piece of paper and wrote the word *No* all over it, covering the front and back of the paper, before finally writing *No more*. Mrs. Bell took this as being bad and sent me with my paper to Mrs. Fox. Mrs. Fox let me stay with her till I settled down while she called my mom. When my mom got there, I was crying. Emma sat with me and hugged me while my mom tried to talk to my teachers. My second-grade teacher just could not understand.

That night, my mom copied part of Temple Grandin's book *Emergence* and sent it to school for my teacher to read. On this paper, Temple explained how she could not listen to music and clap at the same time. My teacher felt that was a problem I would have to deal with and was not her problem. Needless to say, at that moment, my parents knew this was not the school for me. Within another month, my dad had taken another job, and we were moving to Huntsville, where I would finally go to school with my sister.

Learning Different: Mom and Robbie

Trying to figure it out, the million-dollar question. By the time Robbie was seven, we knew he had an unbelievable memory. In spelling tests, he couldn't always hear the punctuation of each word and letter, so he had them memorized. If the teacher was giving the test while walking around and the words for the week may have been *rake*, *lake*, etc., he may had gotten it wrong if the teacher wasn't looking at him when calling out the word. Robbie learned to watch your mouth when you spoke so he could catch the differences in these sounds when they were so close together.

But for the most part, Robbie was an A+ student in spelling and the same with math. Also with facts, the things he could remember that never changed. Reading comprehension was and still is Robbie's hard subject. Robbie reads all day long and is a good reader. But if he just has read a story and you ask him a question like "Why did Tom go to the store?" this would be tough for him. If you ask him "What did Tom buy at the store?" he's got that—milk. But the whys, like maybe it was because the family needed milk or his mother asked him to go or because he wanted to go, all these may have been correct answers, but Robbie's brain is always looking for the one correct answer.

If you ask Robbie who won the Oscars' Best Actress Award, he'll ask which year and can name off every one of them year by year. Just like he was able to drop those alphabet letters in place, once he's seen it, he's got it. But how were we going to get through school? Well, it took a lot of work on Robbie's part and many, many extra hours of homework and modification and patience from his teachers. Most of his teachers saw that Robbie really was a bright child and he could do the work.

Nonetheless, this different way of learning was going to be a challenge, and we were ready to give it our all. The papers, tests, and projects that Robbie came across that he simply could not grasp, we learned to move on from. Yes, earning A or B honor roll was awesome and made him like so many of the other kids, but we also know that the grades were not important; it was the opportunities and making the most of the ones we could.

Mom and Dad would always get frustrated with me, asking, "Robbie, if you can memorize every Disney movie, the names of all the characters, the actor/actress of each voice, and so on, why can't you remember this history material?" I don't really know why it is that I don't remember everything. Maybe it is 'cause I really don't care about all that other stuff. I don't mind reading over and over again anything about Disney or award shows, but not everything interests me enough to read that much.

New School: Robbie

On my first day of school at Challenger Elementary School, I was going to get to meet my new teacher Mrs. McCord. She was so nice to me. When I walked into my new classroom, she was waiting for me and had placed a car eraser and some new pencils, and my name was on the desk. She introduced me to all the students. I was so overwhelmed and needed to just be me for a minute. There was a restroom in our classroom, so I was able to go in there and just unwind for a minute. This was where I could go to stem—this is what they call it when I jump up and down and flap my hands. I don't know why I do this sometimes, but when I get really excited, it just makes me feel better. It's like my way of being excited.

But I knew that not everyone understands why I do this, and it also causes people to stare at me. So I learned to hold it all in till I get home, or here, I had the restroom, where I could go and be me without others staring. When I came out, my parents were still there. They gave me a hug and told me they would be back to get me after school.

Mrs. McCord had us all take a seat at our desk. I looked to my left, and there was a girl named Lauren, and then on my right was another girl that looked just like her, named Megan. They were even wearing the same clothes. They were so nice to me and helped me out all day long, showing me where to go and what to do.

I also got to meet my special education teacher, Mrs. Heater. She was so very nice to me. She told me if I had any problems or needed anything at all, I should just talk to her. Mrs. Heater was so good at helping me solve problems and figure out answers to work I didn't know.

It was important to me that I got the answers right as that meant I had done well. She also let me draw pictures for her.

The other thing that made this school so much better for me was that Emma was there too. I was never able to go to school with Emma before, and I liked her being there with me. If I had any problems, I could just go find her. I loved this new school, my class, my new teacher, and getting to meet new friends. Everyone was so nice to me.

PE in School: Robbie

When I was in second grade, every morning, I would go to a special class called APE (Adaptive Physical Education). I would go to my regular class, and after announcements, I would head down to the gym. However, one morning, I simply did not want to go. There were several other kids in the class with me. Two of them were older boys. These two boys were always mean to my friend in the class. They would pick on him, would call him names, and were mean to him.

We would tell the teacher the things they would say to him, but she never really did anything about it. It was upsetting to me, so I just didn't want to go anymore. I told Mrs. Kachelman, my regular teacher, I didn't want to go and if I could just not stay in class. Mrs. Kachelman told me that I needed to go to class. When I started to get really upset, telling her "No, please, don't make me go," she decided to let me stay with her. I was so relieved not having to go to APE that morning.

That night, Mrs. Kachelman called Mom and Dad to tell them about that morning. Mrs. Kachelman still did not understand why I didn't want to go to class and was calling my parents to let them know what had happened and looking for help on why. Mom and Dad called me into their room and asked me about this. They asked me why I didn't want to go to class. I told them, "Those two boys." They asked me which two and what they did. I told them they were mean, not to me, but to my friend. I started to get upset again, hoping they would not make me go. My parents told me that they would go with me to school tomorrow.

The next morning, Mom and Dad went with me to school and walked down with me to my APE class. They told the teacher they were just there to observe due to the concerns from the day before. While talking to the teacher, they noticed, while the kids were walking a couple of laps around the gym, these two older boys would turn around and say things to Robbie and his friend. My parents pointed this out to the teacher, and she told them that yes, they were not as nice to Robbie's friend, but that they liked Robbie and usually picked Robbie for their team. My mom told the teacher that Robbie was upset because of the way his friend was being treated. Needless to say, I never had to go back to that class again.

My parents went to the front office, made a complaint, and found out what needed to be done because I would not be going back to that class again. Now, it came down to whether the regular PE teacher would allow me into their regular class. And it also required that Mrs. Kachelman would have to change her routine for the whole class in the mornings. The PE teachers, Mrs. Wells, and Dr. Hasty were happy to have me and Mrs. Kachelman make some changes for the class. But it was also all my classmates that were so nice about having me stay with them. Going to the regular PE class was so much fun. The kids were all so nice about helping me, and they would get so excited when I did something good.

The Substitute Teacher: Robbie

I was in third grade at Challenger Elementary School, and Mrs. Mann was my teacher. I really liked Mrs. Mann; she was very nice to me and helped me whenever I needed help. There was this one day when Mrs. Mann was out and our class was in the lunchroom for lunch. The boys at my table were talking too loud while we were to used our quiet voices, and they were messing around with their lunches and throwing things around. I tried to stop them, but they wouldn't listen to me. I took my straw and poked them.

Well, one of the other teachers came up to our table and punished me. I had never seen this teacher before, and I tried to tell her what the boys were doing, but she couldn't understand me and, honestly, wouldn't give me much chance to explain. She made me move to another table all by myself, where I just sat and cried because no one could understand me and I got in trouble because those boys didn't follow the rules. Only bad kids get in trouble, and I didn't want to be a bad kid.

After lunch, Reggie and I went to Mrs. Patterson's, our teacher's, room. I was still really upset, and Reggie explained to Mrs. Patterson what had happened for me. Mrs. Patterson understood why I was upset, and she felt bad for me and hugged me. I just wanted to go home and never come back.

When it was time to go home, I met Emma outside in front of the school. Emma saw that I was still upset and knew something was wrong. Nathan came over and told Emma what happened at lunch. Emma was mad I got punished. When we got home, Emma helped me tell Mom and Dad all about it. Mom was so upset that nobody called her.

So that night, Mom called Mrs. Mann at her home and talked to her about my day and how I didn't want to go back to school. Mrs. Mann felt so bad and asked to speak to me on the phone. She was so nice and said she would take care of everything.

The next day when I walked into school, my friend Devin came up to me and gave me a hug. And just like Mrs. Mann said, when we all got to class, she talked to all the boys, and they all apologized to me. I accepted their apologies, and the teacher that had punished me felt really bad. She wrote me a note saying she was sorry and how much she appreciated me trying to get the boys to behave.

I know some kids get mad at me for always wanting to follow the rules. But they are rules, and you're not supposed to break them. If you break rules, then you are bad. Some of my friends and even my parents will try and get me to what they call bend the rules sometimes. Like when we go to the movies, the rules are to turn your phone off. Mom, Dad, and Emma don't want to turn theirs off, and that's wrong—they are breaking the rules.

Pencil Boy: Robbie

Some of you may know that my parents sometimes call me Pencil Boy. I am guessing this started sometime shortly after we moved to Huntsville. As far back as I can remember, I always loved having with me my toys, like Bugs Bunny and Daffy Duck. Before that, my mom says it was always some Winnie the Pooh figurines. Always having something in my hands gave me something to move around with my fingers.

We always had our pencils at school, and I could keep a pencil with me and not get in trouble. It wasn't long before I always needed to have a pencil in my hand. Sometimes, I wouldn't even know I had it with me, or just having it by me made me feel comfortable.

So I became Pencil Boy, and my dad became Marker Man. I loved to draw and color, and my mom saw that I would sometimes use my drawings to communicate. So I would draw pictures of the character Pencil Boy. It wasn't long before my mom was like, "Robbie, you need to draw a children's picture book of Pencil Boy." So the summer before my fifth-grade year, I made two children's books, *The Adventures of Pencil Boy & Marker Man* and *The Adventures of Pencil Boy & Marker Man: With the Evil 4 Crayons, Stealing King Paper's Crown.* I got to write the story for these books and do all the illustrations.

People have always said I was an artist. Not too long ago, my aunt Beverly asked if I could come stay with her in Baton Rouge and help her do the illustrations for a book she was working on. I was so happy to be able to go help her. I love to draw. It's easy for me, and I just draw what I see. Aunt Beverly gave me a bunch of pictures and wanted me to draw pieces of them together to do the illustrations for her *Kingdom Come: Activities & Fun* book for her church. I enjoy drawing so much that I am willing to draw for anyone who wants me to.

Trip to Disneyland: Robbie

One of my happiest times was when I was able to fly out to Burbank, California, with Dad to visit the animation studios and Disneyland. When I was nine years old, Dad and I were watching TV. I told him I wanted to go to Burbank, California, and my dad responded, "We will go when you turn twelve." So I kept reminding him for two years, "Are we going to Burbank when I turn twelve?" Therefore, I stayed on him about his promise.

So for my twelfth birthday, Dad and I flew out to Burbank, California. We toured all the movie and TV studios and spent one whole day at Disneyland. It was also special because we got to see my cousin Clay. Clay is a writer in Hollywood. He was so nice to take us around on some tours of all the famous places and show us around everywhere.

Clay has always been so awesome. I had done a drawing of Tom Kenny, who is the voice of SpongeBob. Clay told me he might be able to get the drawing I did for Mr. Kenny to him. I couldn't believe this. Not only did Clay do this for me, but also Mr. Kenny mailed me a personal note that he wrote and sent me a CD, an autographed picture, and other stuff on SpongeBob. I still can't believe that Clay did this for me and that Mr. Kenny was so nice to send me a note.

But on our trip to Burbank, we also got to see Mr. Brian, Dad's best friend; he was there on business. We only got to see him for a little bit. But we take a summer trip every other summer with Mr. Brian and his family and Mr. Pete, another one of Dad's friends. I'm not sure what will happen to our summer trips now that Mr. Brian is no longer with us. Mr. Brian is with the angels, and we miss him so much.

Blindsided: Mom

Our fifteen years of public school for Robbie was, for the most part, a success. However, we did have our share of hiccups along the way. The majority of Robbie's teachers did believe in him and put forth extreme efforts to help him succeed. However, there were those few who were hard to work with. One moment to remember was when Robbie was in elementary school, and Rob and I attended our routine IEP (Individual Education Program) meeting. It was rare to get a meeting where all the teachers could attend—regular teachers, resource teachers, APE teachers, OT teachers, and etc. However, on this date, they were all there except for Mr. Houston, the principal, who was off campus at a meeting.

At this meeting, Rob and I were blindsided with information. The teachers stressed that Robbie was not doing well and unhappy. They did not think this was the place (school) for Robbie and that he needed to be at a school that could better handle his issues. Wow. Rob and I were floored. Robbie was unhappy? We had not had any problems getting Robbie to school and had not seen any notes coming home addressing this concern.

On that cue, one of his teachers pulled out a picture that Robbie had drawn two months earlier. Robbie had done a drawing of him and wrote the word *torture* above it. The picture of Robbie was of him sad. My first thought was, *Oh my gosh, what are we missing?* I then noticed the date on the picture and asked why we were just seeing this now. The remaining IEP team proceeded to tell Rob and I that Challenger was an okay fit for Robbie but that Robbie would be better suited for another school that dealt more with the autistic population.

We knew right then that was *not* happening. We asked about aid and assistance and knew one had any real answers. The team went on to tell us that Challenger Middle School would not be the best place for Robbie. This broke our hearts. We chose Challenger because it had the adjoining middle school and would allow for the least bit of transitioning for Robbie. Change schools? Did they realize what they were asking? Autistic children do better without change, and we wanted a school for both our children. They told us that Robbie would be bullied at Challenger Middle and would get eaten alive. What were we hearing?

Robbie had always done so well at Challenger Elementary, receiving awards at all the award presentations, which he worked hard to keep up. What were we going to do? I left this meeting in tears—some of sadness and some of anger. That night, Rob could not sleep. I asked, "What have we done?" We packed up our family and moved eight hours away for a school system where our kids could go to school together. At three o'clock in the morning that night, Rob wrote Governor Riley a letter asking for help. The next day, I started digging, trying to see what might have caused Robbie's drawing back two months earlier. Rob quickly got a reply from Governor Riley's office, which led to a school system meeting.

I found out that the day of Robbie's picture was also an awards day at school. This was the first awards day at his school that he did not receive any kind of award. We tried to explain to Robbie that it was okay not to receive an award, but he just saw it as he had done something wrong. Thus, I could understand his drawing and knew that it was not in reference to how he felt about school. Mr. Houston learned of our IEP meeting and assured us that Challenger Elementary was Robbie's school and he had no intentions of him going anywhere else. After our meeting with head of special ed, we learned that Robbie would be provided the assistance needed to remain intergraded.

To solve the issues that were created about middle school, we decided to take the comments given to us directly to the middle school principal. Rob and I set up a meeting with Mrs. Pickens. We sat down with her and told her of the comments the teachers had about Robbie attending her school and, of course, our concerns as well. She made it very clear that she could not promise us that middle school would work out for Robbie at Challenger but that she could assure us that Challenger Middle School was ready to welcome Robbie with open arms.

We talked about some of the ways we could make the transition for Robbie smoother. One way was that he was currently an office aide for the lower school and could maybe be sent down here to deliver messages to the middle school office, allowing him to get a little more comfortable with the halls and the office staff. Everyone was on board. The lower school would create dummy messages for Robbie to deliver, and the middle school staff got the opportunity to learn who Robbie was. We could not have asked for more.

Rob and I are thankful that we did not take the advice of the teachers during that IEP meeting and trusted our gut. Sometimes it takes tears at meetings or writing letters at three o'clock in the morning or setting up appointments and laying it all out on the table to get to the next step—whatever it takes to give your child a fighting chance.

Great Teachers: Robbie

My last year at Challenger Elementary School was a really special year. I not only got one of the nicest teachers, Mrs. Alley, but I had two special teachers, Mrs. Miller and Mrs. Dull. And that was not all; we also got to spend time in Mrs. Smith's class. Not only did I have this year with so many teachers, but I also had all my friends in my class—Reggie, Buddy, CJ, and Nathan. One of my favorite things about Mrs. Miller's class was a game we played during our spelling test, sparkle.

One of the other things that made this year great was that I got to be an office helper. Every day just before school got out, I would go to the office to help out Mrs. Freeman, Mrs. Leonard, and Mr. Houston. Mr. Houston would always tell me how good of a job I was doing. I would get to help out Mrs. Freeman and Mrs. Leonard by stuffing envelopes and sealing them with a piece of tape. I would also help out by stacking and sorting papers and would deliver things for them all over the school. Emma would have to wait on me till I was done, but then we would get to go home.

A moment that my mom remembers was when she told Mr. Houston once that I really only had one friend, a true friend that would come over and hang out with me. Mr. Houston didn't say anything to my mom, but months later, he mentioned to her that when she told him that, it caught him off guard. All the kids liked me and were so friendly to me at school. He just figured Robbie had tons of friends. So Mr. Houston decided that he was going to be my friend. I love Mr. Houston and miss him. I will always consider him more than my friend.

Angels in the Dark: Robbie

One evening, we were at Grandma's for dinner while visiting family in Baton Rouge. We had since moved to Huntsville, Alabama. Everyone (the Clark side of the family) was at the dining room table sitting around with our desserts. Granddad (Daddy's dad) was brought up, and I, seven to eight years old at the time, made a comment about him. while, everyone at the table was in total shock, put their forks down, got real quiet, and looked at me.

Grandma said, "Well, Robbie, have you seen Granddad?"

I replied, "In my room."

Well, everyone was now on the edge of their seats as Granddad passed away just after Mom and Dad got married in 1990, long before I was even born.

So Daddy asked me, "When?"

I replied, "At night."

Grandma then asked me, "What did Granddad look like?"

I said, "An angel."

I told them how sometimes when I sleep, angels came to see me in my room. They didn't say anything, and my eyes were closed because I am sleeping, but I knew they were there and could see me.

My mom, every once in a while, asks me if I have seen the angels lately, and if she knows of anyone close to us that is sick, hurt, or sad, she asks me to ask the angels if they will look after them for us. She also asks me to ask the angels to help her.

It has been so long since the angels have visited me in my room. But I know they are busy with other people. When I hear that someone has died, I am sad that they are no longer here, but I also know that they are happy and not hurting anymore because they are with the angels. Angels look just like us but have wings and are there to make you feel better.

Tippy-Toes: Robbie

From as far back as I can remember, I have always walked on my tiptoes. People would always ask me why and to put my heels down. I don't know exactly why, but it felt weird on my feet when my whole foot was touching the ground. Walking on my toes puts more pressure on my feet, which feels good to me. My parents always told me to walk with both feet down, but I would only do it when they were watching, then go right back to walking on my tiptoes. I walked on my tiptoes so much that I didn't even know I was doing it.

Then seventh grade came. At that point, my Achilles tendons on both feet were so tight I could not flex my feet enough to get my feet flat on the ground. In seventh grade, I had surgery on both Achilles tendons to release them and allow my feet to have the flexibility to stand flat on the ground. After my surgery, two of my teachers, Ms. Sullivan and Ms. Eison, came to my house with balloons and a cake. I was so surprised to see them. They came to my house to see me and made sure I was okay.

Both of my legs were in casts for six weeks. But in the end, I was able to put my feet flat on the ground. I have to say, the casts drove me crazy. They itched so badly. I would shove my pencils down inside them to try and scratch my legs as much as possible. The cotton around the top of the cast itched so bad I pulled it all off, leaving the rough edge of the cast rubbing against my legs. Shoving the pencil inside the cast also made the cotton deep down bundle up in spots. Therefore, after a couple weeks, I ended up getting rub marks from the top of the cast and cast burns on my heels.

When I went in to see Dr. Buckley, he told the nurse to take them off and clean up my sore spots, but then he would have to put them back on for the last three weeks. I wasn't happy about that, but for those few minutes in between where I got to itch my legs and have my sore spots wrapped, it was a great feeling.

Since the surgery, castings, and rehab, I now know how to walk with both my feet down. Sometimes I still roll up on my toes; I just can't help it. My calf muscles have become so strong over the years, and my parents still keep an eye on me to make sure I'm not on my toes.

Coming to Grips: Dad

I was always concerned my wife was being overprotective of Robbie as he was becoming a teenager. It was only natural to want to protect your child from harm. As Robbie became older, I too found myself trying to make sure his day to day was simple and without issue. My biggest fear was that he would be forced into some situation he couldn't handle and have a meltdown. It took a conscious effort to let him just be him. This meant allowing him to make his own decisions and possibly mistakes that would have consequences.

At some point in Robbie's life, he will face adversity different than what he has on a day-to-day basis. It is healthy for all of us to face this adversity head-on. I'm feeling more and more confident Robbie will be just fine when that day comes. He is no different than any other twenty-two-year-old in that regard which has some level of comfort in knowing they are all in it together.

Friends and Homework: Robbie

Growing up, I only had one friend, Devin, who would come over to my house and play. However, Emma would always have friends over, and she would let me play with them. One of my favorite things to play was tree tag. We played this all the time with Cassidy, Crystal, and Devin, the little boy who lived behind us. We would have to get to the tree before being tagged while running back and forth on the trampoline. I also loved jumping on the trampoline.

Emma always had lots of friends over, and they would let me play with them and be so nice to me. Sometimes they would go to Emma's room and play in there, but that was okay, 'cause I liked just being in my room too. When I would get home from school, I couldn't wait to go to my room and see all my Disney characters. I have little stuffed animals of just about all of them. I would also play back on my computer some of my favorite episodes. These Disney characters were like my own friends.

My mom was always good about giving me some time to unwind before asking me to start my homework. I didn't mind doing my homework because I didn't want to get in trouble at school for not doing it. I also wanted to do what was right. My mom and dad would have to help me because I didn't understand some of it.

First-grade class at Westminster with the teacher, Mrs. Anderson

With Ben (my brother) at one of our
crawfish boils in Huntsville, Alabama

With Devin, after Devin had moved
away and I had graduated, 2013

Graduation crawfish boil with Scotty,
JD, Hayden, and Allie

Mrs. Sullivan at my graduation

At the HSV Museum of
Art with my artwork

With Reggie after our eighth-grade graduation

With Ali McGraw

With Temple Grandin

Receiving my award at the CMS Basketball Banquet

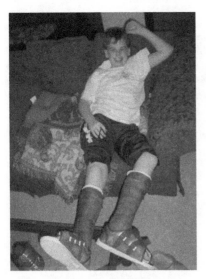

After surgery in
seventh grade

At graduation,
waving at family

With Mrs. Pickens in eighth grade

At the senior banquet that Hayden took me to

With Hayden after graduation

Meme and Papaw at my graduation dinner

With Grandma at my graduation dinner

With Dad when I was about two years old

At Walt Disney Studios for my twelfth-birthday
trip to Burbank, California, with Dad, 2005

Me (left), Cousin Kyle (center) and Cousin Mike (right)

With Kyle and Mike 20 years later

Stoney and Lucy, my dogs   With Lori, my therapist

With my Mom

With Emma, 2012   With Emma, 1997

In Baton Rouge reading my Disney books

With Biscuit 2001

With Mr. Houston at the
fifth-grade graduation

With Cousin Clay

With Cameron at a Grissom Pep Rally, 2012

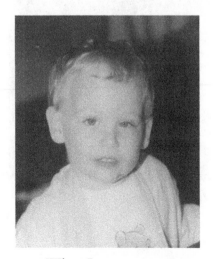

When I was younger

When I dressed up as Mickey
Mouse for little kids

My family frying turkeys, Thanksgiving 2014

It's Great to Have Friends: Robbie

Not everyone is nice. When I was in the sixth grade, after PE class, everyone was changing back into their clothes. I was trying to hurry up so I would not be late to class. I did not like being late. I always made sure to go straight to my classes and not talk to anyone so I wouldn't be late.

One day, some boys were in the locker room when everyone was getting changed, and they took my clothes from me. They kept throwing them back and forth and wouldn't give them back. I tried to stop them. They were laughing at me. I got so furious and wanted to cry. They finally gave me my clothes back. I told the coaches about it, but a couple of days later, they did it again.

Later that day, my friend Devin came to me and asked me what happened. After I told him what happened, he hugged me to make me feel better. He told me if they did anything to me again, I should just go talk to him. Other kids told me that Devin and my other friend Reggie made sure those boys didn't bother me again.

That same day after school, before I could even get to the car, some of my other friends, Megan, Lauren, and Allie, all ran to my mom's car and told her what had happened. My mom was really upset and went with me to school the next day to talk to the principal, Mrs. Pickens. Mrs. Pickens was so nice and glad that my mom told her what had happened. She said she would make sure it was handled. She gave security officer Mr. Melillo my schedule and made sure he was present on the halls where I would be when changing classes to keep an eye out. I can say I never had any more problems with those boys.

Dodgeball: Robbie

When I was at Challenger Middle School, we would have gym class every day. My coaches were Coach Dodson and Coach Lee. Some of the games we would play were hard for me. I would always try my hardest to do them, but I didn't run as fast as some of the other kids, and sometimes it would hurt my arm to throw the balls. But dodgeball, I loved this game. It was so much fun watching everyone run around and funny watching everyone try not to get hit.

We would always have to start out by doing little exercises before we could play. Coach Lee and Coach Dodson would let me pick up all the balls and put them on the line to start. Everyone would try to hit someone. I tried to get the ball and try to hit someone and get him or her out, but I usually missed. Actually, it was me that always got hit and out. I loved this game and always had so much fun playing.

Every Friday in PE, we got to play dodgeball. I would have to play whatever else Coach Lee and Coach Dodson wanted me to play, but on Fridays we would play dodgeball. I made sure to always follow the rules, and when I graduated from eighth grade, I was given a dodgeball award. I was so surprised and excited to get this award.

A couple years later, when talking to my sister, Emma told me how they were not allowed to play dodgeball at school anymore. In fact, I found out that my class was the only class that got to play dodgeball at all, much less every Friday. Coach Lee and Coach Dodson must have really liked me to let me do this even when we weren't supposed to. Maybe it was because I made sure we all followed the rules. I would watch everyone to make sure that they all followed the rules.

Proud Sister: Emma

Every day I am proud to be Robbie's sister. All through school, it was, "You're Robbie's little sister? I love Robbie." There wasn't one day when I wouldn't proudly say he was my brother. He was the kind of person that cheered everyone up, and everyone in the school knew him—everyone. And anyone who knew Robbie knew his smile and how contagious it was.

Anyway, there is one day that stands out more than others, though. When Robbie was in eighth grade (I was in seventh), he was able to be a basketball manager for our school's basketball team. The whole middle school gathered in the gym for a pep rally. This pep rally was the one where they introduced the team for the beginning of their season. The whole team was being announced, and I was so excited Robbie was getting to be a part of this. I was sitting there cheering for everyone, and then they said, "Robbie Clark!" My face just lit up so incredibly, and I screamed with all my soul. I stopped for a second to catch my breath and to watch him gallop out like he does when he gets excited and wave to everyone.

I was in shock at how loud every single person in the gym was cheering, all for Robbie. No one else could compete with the noise people made for Robbie. My stomach got the butterflies because I was just so happy for him. He had the biggest smile on his face, and in that moment, I sat there and was in awe.

"That's my brother. How lucky am I to say I am Robbie Clark's little sister."

All my friends sitting with me were just smiling and hitting me.

"This is awesome, Emma."

"I'm so happy for him."

"I love Robbie."

Ball Boy: Robbie

I was a ball boy for Challenger's basketball team. My eighth-grade year, Coach Dodson, the basketball coach, asked me if I would like to help out with the basketball team. I wasn't sure what he was asking but knew I didn't want to play basketball. But he wanted to see if I would help out when they had home games. Coach Dodson needed help making sure that none of the basketballs were lost and that there were always cups of water filled for the boys. I told him I would do it, but I will say I was nervous at first.

So whenever they had a home game, I would stay after school and make sure to keep up with all the balls. There were a lot of balls, and they would go everywhere, but I made sure that they all were put back on the rack before the game started. I would also fill up the cups of water for all the boys. I would have to help put out the chairs before and after the game. Everyone said I was really good at being the manager. However, the best was getting to run out with the team during the pep rally. When they called my name, I got to run out and line up with all the boys. I was so excited and waved to everyone. I also, got to go to the end-of-the-season banquet. I was so surprised when Coach Dodson said so many nice things about me. He called my name, and I got to go up on the stage and get an award. I was so proud and happy to be a part of their team.

Who's Joe?: Robbie

One day in class, Ms. Sullivan thought she would be funny by calling me Joe. All the kids laughed, and I could not understand why they were laughing at me. Why would calling me Joe be so funny? It made me mad when she called me Joe. She continued to call me Joe and, everyone continued to laugh. Sometimes people need to understand that something they think is funny might frustrate someone else. Because I was mad, I figured I would start calling her Ms. Joe. People laughed when I did that, but it didn't make Ms. Sullivan mad; in fact, she just laughed. This made me even madder. I know Ms. Sullivan never meant to make me frustrated or mad.

Over time, it became the joke, and others would start calling me Joe too. I didn't know how to get them to stop. I would tell them "My name is not Joe," but it didn't stop them. I would make mad faces, and nothing worked. I would tell them "That's not my name," but everyone just thought it was funny. I just learned to go along with it as good as I could even though I didn't like it or understand why anyone would call me Joe anyway.

Several years later, I still get mad when people call me Joe or anything other than my name, Robbie. Just like my aunt Kat. She will sometimes call me Robster. Why does she do that? Mom said that sometimes people just have their own nicknames for people, like we call Emma as Em. But I don't like that; my name is Robbie, and Emma's name is Emma.

Stoney (Jimmie) Clark: Robbie

Several months after Biscuit (my first dog) had died, my mom asked Emma and me if we wanted to look at getting a new dog. Even though all I really wanted was to have Biscuit back, I knew that wasn't going to happen. He was an angel in heaven now. So one day after school, we went by the Human Society, an animal shelter here in town. There were so many dogs and cats. They keep the dogs and cats in separate areas, so we only looked at the dogs.

All the dogs were barking and going crazy trying to get our attention. Emma really liked this brown puppy that had one blue eye and one brown eye. That puppy was going crazy. They let him out so we could see him, and he was jumping all over the place. After we looked at all the dogs outside and inside twice, I finally found one that caught my eye. He was in a cage by himself, and he just laid there. He wasn't jumping around, barking, or anything. He had such a sad face. The shelter said his name was Stoney, and he had been there for over ten months. His face was so sad.

When they let him out for us to see him, all he did was lay at our feet and put his head down. He was so sad. I looked into his eyes, and they were beautiful. I knew right then he was the one. We called Dad right away 'cause the shelter was about to close and I didn't want to leave Stoney there. I wanted him to come home with us right then. Dad said yes, and we filled out all the paperwork and brought Stoney home!

Special Award: Robbie

In eighth grade, I had a teacher named Mrs. Driskill. She was my English teacher. Mrs. Eaton was another teacher that I had for learning strategies. Mrs. Eaton would go into our English class with us and help us later in her class when we needed it. One day, we had a spelling test in Mrs. Driskill's class, and then we got to go back to our class with Mrs. Eaton, where she would give us a chance at some bonus words.

I usually did really well on my spelling test, as they were easier for me. After I had the opportunity to see the words a couple of times, I could just remember them. But when some of the words would sound the same, then it would be harder, as sometimes I couldn't always hear the difference in them.

However, on this date, I remember getting a 105 percent on my test. I was so excited. But nothing surprised me more than when Mrs. Driskill called my name for a special award at our eighth-grade graduation. When she called out my name, I jumped up and hurried to the stage, where I got to go across to get my award. I couldn't wait to get to her and give her a hug. I looked over and saw Mrs. Eaton with a big smile on her face.

After the awards ceremony I saw Mom and Dad. Mom was crying, and I could tell Dad had been crying too. They said it was because they were so happy for me, but I don't know why that would make them cry. When I showed Emma my award, she was so proud of me. I was happy to have received this special award from Mrs. Driskill. I will never forget her.

Part of the Village: Mom

Keeping up with all the different classes once Robbie reached middle and high school was quite difficult. In middle school, they had a weekly calendar that was used by all students and allowed plenty of room for notes from teachers for each class. Robbie's routine with his special education teacher was to stop by her room before leaving each day to make sure his daily calendar was filled out and that he had all his assignments. This was so important in allowing us to know what would be expected of him.

When moving into high school, this system that we had developed in middle school was something we wanted to continue. After having trouble finding a daily planner that allowed the room for each class's notes, we contacted Robbie's old principal from middle school, Mrs. Pickens, and asked if they may have an extra planner that Robbie could buy. This may have seemed as something very trivial to her but made things so much simpler for us.

As much as this planner was a lifesaver for us in keeping all Robbie's classes and assignments in order, it still didn't always cover everything. An example, in English in tenth grade, Robbie came home with a packet (ten to twelve back-to-back pages) of work sheets. All his planner had down was "Complete work sheets." You can imagine the shock when I saw this large packet of work sheets and thought there was no way we can get all this done in one night. I asked Robbie about the assignment, and all he had was that it was due tomorrow.

This was when I started asking Robbie who were some of the other kids in his class. As soon as he named off a kid we had a phone number for, Tripp, we called him to find that only a couple of pages of this packet was actually due. What a relief this was to know that all the pressure wasn't on Robbie to get every detail, that we had backups. I can assure you we called on Tripp many times.

You can also get some of these names at your child's open house, where the parents show up to meet the teacher. In our case, meeting some of the other parents was just as important. So get names and phone numbers of other kids. They will become part of your village.

Voting: Dad

I remember turning eighteen and going with my dad to register to vote. He stressed how important it was and that it was a God-given right to be able to vote in this great country. That had such an impressionable impact on me, and I felt I should share this same experience with my son like I had done with my father. I was proud of him for doing it and for voting in his first presidential election. He said he didn't know whom to vote for and wanted me to just tell him whom to mark. I was adamant that he came with his own conclusion on whom to vote for in the election.

It was fun watching him make his decision on whom to vote for in each position. I am pretty sure he picked the name that he could associate with each contest based on how many people had the same name and either worked at Disney or in the film industry. Hey, he voted, and that's what matters. He fulfilled a family pastime that has been handed down for generations now.

The Principal: Robbie

My mom told me that Mr. Houston, our principal, was going to retire. They were going to have a big party for him at the school, where everyone can come out and talk to him. A couple of days later, a lady called my mom and asked if I wouldn't mind being part of a video they were making for Mr. Houston. I was so excited about being able to tell Mr. Houston just how much I loved him.

A guy who was making the video came to my high school, where Devin and I met him in the main office. He had us sit down, and when he was recording, we were able to say a message to Mr. Houston. I wasn't prepared and didn't know what I wanted to say. And I actually don't remember what all I said, but I hope I told him just how much I love him.

Mr. Houston was always so nice to me. He would always smile at me and tell me how good of a job I was doing. I don't know everything he did for me, but I do know that my mom and dad told me that if it weren't for Mr. Houston, I probably would not have made it through school. He spoke up for me when some of my teachers didn't believe in me. I will always love Mr. Houston and miss seeing him.

Unexpected Changes: Robbie

Grissom was a really big school. Every summer before school started, my mom would always take me by so we could go over my schedule. I was able to practice walking to and from classes and going to my locker. However, one year, my sophomore year, I was in Coach Utley's class when Coach gave me a new schedule. I didn't know what was going on. I didn't want a new schedule; I didn't need a new schedule. I didn't know what to do.

Coach Utley didn't know anything about it and let me go see Mrs. Porter, my counselor. When I got to her office, I was so confused and upset. Coach Tate had wanted me in his learning strategies class, but even though I really liked Coach Tate, I didn't want to change any of my classes. This was simply too big of a change for me. Mrs. Porter could see just how upset I was and let me stay in her office all afternoon till something could be worked out.

To switch classes and teachers now was not even an option. No, I wasn't going to do it. Mrs. Porter and Coach Tate understood and undid all the changes to my schedule, leaving me in all my current classes. I liked all my current classes and teachers and knew all who were in my classes. I also already knew where to go and what to do. So I was so happy to just keep things the same and not have any changes.

Having that time before school to prepare for where my classes would be and learn about my teachers really did help me.

Downtime: Robbie

I know I spend a lot of time in my room. But this is where I feel most comfortable. If I am sad, have a bad day, or excited and happy, I just go to my room, where I can let things out and be myself. I love spending time on my computer. I like to look up information about things I am interested in so I can learn everything possible. I will also talk to myself a lot while in my room. I can talk about the things that are bothering me and/or things I may be excited about. I also love drawing pictures. I have drawn tons of pictures of all the Disney characters and of all the Disney movies.

Being in my room, I will think about all the good and bad memories I have. I love to watch any of the Disney film clips on YouTube; I love watching clips of my favorite shows. I will also do lots of reading. I have read just about everything there is on Disney, Oscars, and other award shows. One of the first things I check when I get on my computer is the Wikipedia site.

I hate seeing when anyone whom I know or have read about dies. However, if it is an actor or actress, then I will research them and learn about everything they had accomplished in their life. My mom and dad think it's amazing that I can always remember all this information. It interests me, and I like learning all about them and the movies, so I read everything over and over again.

Angel in the Making: Robbie

I know when you die, you get to go to heaven and you will get to be an angel and watch over everyone. Angels are very special. A couple of years ago, one of my math teachers, Coach Massey, died. He was such a nice man. I was so sad to hear that he was sick. When my mom came in my room and told me that Coach Massey had died, I was very sad but didn't cry 'cause I knew he was with the angels and was not going to hurt anymore.

I was lucky enough to get to visit Coach Massey at his house before he passed away. I got to meet his wife and give her a card I drew and a note that I wrote for him. He was kind of asleep when I was there to visit him, but Mrs. Massey told him I was there. He held on to my hand and squeezed it tight. I had gotten my glasses since the last time I had seen him, so I hoped he would recognize me.

It had been a couple of years, but at the end of my ninth-grade year, when I had Coach Massey as my teacher, he wrote my parents a note for me to give them after my exam. My parents were so touched by the note he had handwritten to them about me. Therefore, my mom told me that it was only fitting that I do the same for him now.

A few days later, Coach Massey died. The day before his memorial service, which my family and I had planned to attend, one of Coach Massey's friends called me and asked if it would be okay if they read my note to him at his memorial service. I was so happy that my letter meant that much to Coach Massey and his family. When they read my note at the service, I was really sad, but I didn't cry because I knew Coach Massey was looking down on me and smiling.

What Big Brothers Do: Emma

Growing up I might have been Robbie's little sister, but to me, the role was reversed. I was the one looking out for him, making sure he was always okay, and helping him do simple tasks, and for most of the time, I would tell myself I was really the older one, until this day. Robbie and I both had to get our wisdom teeth out, and my parents decided "Why not just get them out at the same time?" (even though mine weren't quite ready). So Robbie, my parents, and I went to the doctor's office one morning and waited patiently for both of our procedures.

Honestly, I was terrified and did not want to go first, but I didn't want Robbie to be scared, so I needed to show him it would be okay. The lady came out to ask which one of us wanted to go first, and we both said "I will," and I was just quiet. I asked, "Robbie, are you sure? I can go first." And he said, "No I'll go."

He had this look of confidence on his face even though I knew he was terrified. You must be thinking, *Why does this mean so much to her?* My whole life, every little moment has been helping Robbie, making sure he understands everything and making sure he gets where he needs to be. But that moment, I truly realized we are just like every other set of siblings and I don't need to worry about him so much anymore. He has learned to do so many things I don't have to help him with anymore.

Honestly, in a way, it almost confused me because I love helping my brother because he is so grateful. Helping him has taught me more than anyone could imagine. There are things like driving him, helping him with money, understanding people in public, and all the other little things he has learned. It might take him longer to do it or take longer to learn, but he's finally gotten there. Ever since that moment, I never say to myself I'm older. I might be able to handle things by myself, but my brother will protect me.

Drawing and Art: Robbie

I have always been the kid that loved to draw. Drawing was an early way for me to communicate when I couldn't find the words or when people simply could not understand me. Drawing was something I was good at, and I don't know, but I could see the image or picture and how it should be. I also had a way of remembering all the details of things, and when I would draw them, I would include all these details that I could still see in my mind.

When middle school came and I would be given an opportunity to take an art class, I was so excited. In sixth grade, it wasn't an option. I had to take either band or choir, neither of which I wanted to take. These classes were hard for me as all the noise was horrible for me. My ears were really sensitive, and it would hurt my ears to be in places where there were lots of loud sounds. In seventh grade, I was able to sign up for art. This was, by far, my favorite class ever. I had finally found a class that I felt comfortable with.

I was so glad to know that there was also an eighth-grade art class. For this class, it was up to the teacher if I could take the class. I do not know why, but I was not let into the class. I remember the day as Mom was in shock and so upset when she got the news that the teacher was not going to let me in her class. School was so hard for me, and art was the one thing that I got and loved. I had loved going to art all year and now wasn't going to have it anymore.

Not being let into art in eighth grade was just like so many other times in my life. Like when I was a preschooler and many schools not taking me because I didn't fit in. To me, this was a way of people telling me I was not good enough. So for this year, I went back to just drawing in my room on my own by myself.

When I got to Grissom High School, the angel of Mrs. Huffstetler was a dream. She welcomed me into her class year after year. She always encouraged me to express myself through my art. She showed me how to see shadows, lights, darks, depth, and so much more. She was so nice to me and made me feel special. When my senior year came along, the only way I could take art was if the teacher would be willing to work me into one of her classes as an independent study. After my experience in eighth grade, I was scared that this same thing would happen again. But Mrs. Huffstetler told my adviser that she would be more than happy to have me as an independent-study student and would fit me into her schedule whenever it was needed.

This was one of the most amazing years of art. Since I was doing my own study, I got to work on my own projects during Mrs. Huffstetler's class. She would work with me on different ideas and help me with my drawings. I got to paint several different pieces, some of which my mom has up in the house today. I also got to make figurines and bowls out of clay. I am so thankful to Mrs. Huffstetler and will never forget her.

One Great Accomplishment: Robbie

The end of my senior year of high school was finally getting close. Every year since we moved here to Huntsville, we have held a crawfish boil. Our friends and family would help bring crawfish up to us: Ben, Joey, Joe, Kyle, Mike, even Uncle Doug. So this year, it was going to be a special crawfish boil for my graduation. I couldn't believe I was finally going to be done with school and was going to graduate. There were also a lot of other people who wouldn't believe I was able to do it either.

My mom sent out graduation cards to everyone, letting them know that I did it. So many people came. They all brought me cards and told me just how happy and proud they were of me. I invited some of my friends—Allie, Scotty, Hayden, and his brother JD. It was so nice to be just like them and to see just how many people were proud of me. I gave everyone a hug and told them "Thank you!" But my mom and dad tell me that we will never be able to really thank everyone who has truly been a part of my graduation.

Nonetheless, I will take this time to once again say thank you.

That day of graduation, I will never forget. Lots of my family from Baton Rouge made the trip to Huntsville just to see me graduate. I got dressed and put on my brown cap and gown, and Emma and Hunter took me to the Von Braun Civic Center since I had to get there early. I was kind of nervous. I had never graduated before, and even though we practiced, I didn't want to mess anything up.

When we took our seats, I was actually seated on the end and saw where my mom and dad where seated pretty fast. Mr. Ben was there, Grandma, Meme, Papaw, Aunt Kat, Aunt Sharon, Aunt Bev, Cousin

Katie, Cousin MaryBeth, Sam, Laura, and several of Emma's friends by her and Hunter all there to see me. And then out of the corner of my eye, I saw Ms. Sullivan. She had a big smile on her face. She was yelling my name and holding up a sign she made. It was a Mickey Mouse head, and it said Way to Go, Joe! I still have this sign in my room today. It also has on the other side Robbie 2012! I could see just how happy she was for me.

It wasn't long before they started calling all our names. It was time for me to walk across the stage. I heard them call my name, and I was so excited. I hurried across the stage looking at all my classmates as they clapped and screamed for me. I waved at them all and shook Mr. Drake's hand. Then I saw Mrs. Pickens; she was waiting to give me a hug. I then hurried off the stage and saw all my family standing up, waving at me. Everyone had big smiles on their faces. I will never forget that day.

Rafting, Anyone?: Robbie

After I graduated from high school, we took a trip to go white-water rafting and zip lining. It was going to be me, Mom, Emma, and Hunter. Dad had work, so he and the three boys that were spending the summer with us—Anthony, Jordan, and Steven—would have to meet us there later that night. So me, Mom, Emma, and Hunter went zip lining. This was the first time for me to do this. It was so much fun. My mom was scared, but I wasn't. I would jump off as far as I could and loved going fast.

Mom and Emma were surprised that I wasn't scared, but I wasn't. I would jump and hoot like Goofy. It was like I was getting to be like Goofy, and I loved it. After we were done zip lining, we went to this hotel that was like a cabin to stay the night. We were really tired but wanted to stay up till Dad and the boys got there. They finally made it after getting lost in the mountains on the way. They were so funny when they got there talking about how scary it was being lost on the dark roads.

The next day we got up early, got breakfast, and headed out to go white-water rafting. I had already gone white-water rafting before with my cousins Kyle and Mike and my aunt Kat and uncle Wendell. It was so much fun. All us guys got our own boat (me, Dad, Uncle Wendell, Kyle, Mike, and Wes). Mom, Emma, and Aunt Kat got another boat with some other people they didn't know. I had such a great time, but Aunt Kat fell out of her boat, and she did not like that at all. Anyhow, after breakfast, with all the boys, we headed to go rafting. This time, Mom got the boat with the three boys, and me, Dad, Emma, and Hunter had our own boat. This was also Hunter's first time to go rafting, and he loved it. Everyone had such a good time. I love zip lining and rafting and can't wait to go again.

Senior Banquet: Robbie

Senior year of high school, all the seniors had a party called the Senior Banquet. I was so excited about going but didn't want my mom or dad taking me as no one else's parents took them. My friend Hayden offered to pick me up and take me. I was so excited about going but also about being able to go with Hayden. Everyone likes Hayden; he is so nice to everyone. When we got to the party, we got good seats and had dinner. Everyone was talking and having such a good time.

My friends were glad to see me and glad that I came. I gave all of them a good hug 'cause I love them all. They had a video to show and some awards for some of the seniors. I was in the video in one of the pictures with Cameron. After everyone was done eating, watching the video, and giving out awards, everyone wanted to take pictures with their phones. I was asked to be in some of them, which made me happy. When everyone was done taking pictures, Hayden brought me home. It was late, but I had such a great time getting to see everyone. I miss all of them. I don't miss going to school, but I do miss seeing all my friends.

I Feel Responsible: Emma

Robbie and I, at one time, decided to go parasailing while at the beach. I was going into my senior year of high school, and he had just graduated. Our dad drove us to the location for the ride. Once we got there, we realized Dad was not going to be able to go with us. Instantly, I didn't want to go. One, I was nervous, and two, I didn't know how Robbie was going to do, and I felt all this sudden responsibility so fast. Dad being Dad said, "Grow up and go enjoy it."

So off Robbie and I went on a boat full of strangers. The whole time, Robbie was smiling, with the wind blowing through his hair. I was sitting there trying to enjoy it, but I get seasick easily, so I tried to focus on not getting sick. Robbie could tell I was really uptight, and he just put his arm around me, and I knew it is going to be well worth it. Eventually, I asked this girl, probably my age, who was sitting next to us if she would take pictures of us if I gave her my phone, and she said, "Of course."

So it was our turn to go, and we were sitting on the edge of the boat, and off we went. Robbie was making the "Weeeeeahhhhhwahooo" noise that he makes. Everyone on the boat was just looking at us two going off, and the girl was taking pictures of us. I started to wonder if they could tell Robbie has a disability or if they just thought he was weird. I didn't care. I just didn't want them talking bad about him.

We got to the top, and when Robbie was really excited, he started swaying, leaning front and back like on a swing. So I was not really enjoying this experience. I didn't mind it, but when Robbie was moving back and forth, it made me a little uneasy. So I said anxiously, "Robbie, can we stay really still?" He said, "Oops, sorry. Yes, Emma." He could tell I was scared, but once we stopped moving, I calmed down.

The whole time, I could just tell Robbie felt free, and I was trying to make sure he had fun and make sure nothing would happen to make him uncomfortable when, truthfully, I was just worrying way more than I should. Robbie and I landed back on the boat, got unhooked, and went to sit down. The girl that had my phone took such good pictures. I could see the excitement and relaxed feeling Robbie had on his face. I thought to myself it was worth it. Robbie and I did something just the two of us.

I don't want to feel like I need to worry about Robbie all the time because he is capable of being on his own. It's just my natural instinct to do so. As I've gotten older, I try to tell myself that and let Robbie do what he wants, not telling him what to do. Sometimes he says "Stop telling me what to do, Emma," and it really hurts me because I don't want him to think that's what I am doing. I never mean it that way. I normally mean it in a "Why don't you try this instead."

Every time I go home, I try to tell myself to not be that way, and I have gotten better. I hope he notices it. This, over time, has brought me to think Robbie probably feels this way all the time from his friends, classmates, coworkers, teachers, and everyone. They don't even notice it, just like me, but we tend to feel we need to take care of him and tell him what to do. But we don't.

Yes, sometimes we do, but so does everyone. I want society to know just because someone is disabled doesn't mean you should treat them differently. You should treat them with the same independence you feel you should be treated. I think this is a problem with anyone who knows a person with a disability, but like I said, it's our instinct. But truthfully, they can do it on their own, and we need to let them, encourage them, and remind them that they can.

Things That Scare Me: Robbie

I get scared and nervous whenever I am thrown out of my routine and forced to try something new or attempt to do something that is not in my typical routine. For example, when I was sixteen, my mom wanted me to go take the test to get a driver's permit. I was scared to take the test because if I passed, I would begin to drive, and people who drive get in accidents, and people who get in accidents can die. Therefore, it was easy for me to avoid driving. I have taken the written driving exam several times but have failed it each time. I think if I really tried, I could have passed it, but all I could think about when studying the booklet was *accidents*. This scares me.

Money makes me nervous. I have a hard time counting money, and therefore, I get nervous when I have to deal with it. What if I don't have enough? What if I give back the wrong number? What if they look at me funny? In my perfect world, there would not be any money. The idea of having to pay bills makes me nervous. I have a job, and I make money with tips, but I don't use any of it. All my money goes into the bank in savings. Dad makes me keep ten to twenty dollars in my wallet in case of emergencies or just in case I want to get something to eat or drink. My parents tell me I need to keep saving my money so that one day I will hopefully be able to take care of myself that I will need every penny I can save.

Insects are very scary too. I hate when they fly around me. It makes me very stressed. The fear of being stung by a wasp makes me scared to go outside sometimes. When I was little, I got stung by a wasp, and it hurt. I would rather stay inside all the time; however, my job requires me to work outside all the time. My parents also have me take the dogs for walks too. So if those bugs come around me, I just get away from them as quick as I can.

I still have these fears, but over the years, they have gotten a lot better. Not only have I learned to do things that used to scare me but also new things that I never really thought about. Roller coaster is something that never really scared me, but I would be nervous. But there are some rides that may make me sick, like ones that go in circles real fast.

Award Shows: Robbie

When I am on my computer learning all about the Disney movies, I start taking notice at the awards the movies have won. This leads to actors'/actresses' awards and so on. So I start learning more about this show called the Academy Awards, a.k.a. the Oscars. It is a movie award for best films, best actors, best actresses, best directors, and many more.

So that year, I watched the Oscars with Dad, and it was great. I was able to remember all the movies, actors, actresses, directors, etc., they were talking about. So from that year on, we would print out the list of all the nominations and pick which we thought would win. I started taking these printouts to school so all my teachers and friends could pick who they thought would win too.

After learning as much as I could about the Oscars, I found some other award shows: Golden Globe Awards for movie and television awards; Primetime Emmy Awards for primetime television awards; Daytime Emmy Awards for daytime television awards; and Annie Awards for animation awards. So I started to learn as much as I could about all these shows. Everyone tells me that I know everything about Disney and any award shows.

I don't know why I don't know as much about money and school stuff like I do Disney and awards, but I do. Those other things just don't interest me. I don't care about them. I know how to find on the computer all kinds of information on these topics, and I love reading it all. For some reason, I can remember all these facts, dates, people, and information. After I have read and seen it, I can just remember it. I love being able to know everything about Disney and the award shows. I really love them.

I can't explain how, but I can recite any winner of any Academy Award ever won in the history of the Academy Awards. It is just something I enjoy learning about.

Dog's Best Friend: Robbie

Even though I told everyone I didn't like school, it was mainly because some of the classes were hard for me. But I did like getting to see my friends every day. I would always get excited when school let out for summer because that was what everyone else was doing—getting excited. Every summer while school was out, I loved being able to sleep in and not have homework, but I would also get lonely.

I was so glad that I had my dog, Biscuit, but he died in 2007, on the same day I had surgery on both my legs. I still miss him so much every day. I now have Stoney and Lucy; they are good at keeping me company. Whenever my parents are gone for work or have plans with Emma, then I would have my dogs to watch after. They keep me company while I play on my computer, watch movies, and think about things.

My dogs have now become more of my friends since I have graduated. I really miss my friends—Devin, Mitch, Hayden, and all my other friends. My friend Austin was able to make sure I got an invitation to his wedding. He even messaged me on Facebook to make sure I got the invitation. I loved getting to go to this, what a happy day, as I really love Austin and Madeline so much. I do have some of my friends' cell phone numbers so they can call or text me if anything comes up. I am lucky to have such good friends and so many people love me.

But I don't have friends like Emma's. When we were little, Emma always had friends over, and not just one friend, but bunches of them. She would also get asked to go with them to their house and to go places with them. I do remember when I was in elementary school, Devin did invite me to his house for a party, where all the boys came over. This was fun. I didn't stay the night but did have fun playing with them.

Loss of Friends: Robbie

I have to take a moment to tell you about my friend Tyreez. Tyreez went to school with me at Challenger; however, I didn't get to know him that well until Challenger Middle School. In middle school, I had Tyreez in several of my classes. There was a group of friends—Devin, Buddy, Cameron, CJ, Reggie, Nathan, Perry, Dannyell, and Ben—that had a lot of classes together, and we got to know each other really good.

I knew I would try to help out any of these boys if I could. Even when they would not follow directions, I would tell them to stop and try and help them so they wouldn't get in trouble. They also helped me out a lot whenever I needed help. Tyreez was one of the boys that would help me out in class and would always speak to me in the halls and be my friend. I was so sad when I heard Ty had died in a car accident. Tyreez was too young to die, and I miss him.

It is so sad when I hear that someone else has died. I also remember when we got the news that Hogan Vaughn had died in a car accident as well. Cassidy, Emma's best friend and Hogan's cousin, was at our house when her mom called late at night. I could hear Cassidy crying and Emma getting my mom. I felt so bad for Cassidy. She was so sad, and everyone was crying so hard. Hogan and Tyreez are still with us as they are now angels.

Another loss that was very hard was when Hunter's dad died. I felt so bad for Hunter as he was so sad and you could see how much he was hurting. When his dad was in the hospital and Hunter would not leave the hospital, Emma would not leave either. Me, Mom, and Dad would take turns bringing food up to them at the hospital.

I remember one time when we went up to the hospital to bring dinner for Hunter, his brother Walker, and Ms. Teresa. We were sitting in the lobby waiting for Hunter to come get the food from us. When Hunter came down the elevator, he just started crying so hard and wouldn't let go of Emma. Dad and Mom started crying. This hurt my heart. I asked the angels to let Hunter's dad stay here with Hunter longer. I had only met Mr. George a few times, but I love Hunter, and it was hard to see him so sad. I wish people didn't have to die, but I know they are happy and not hurting in heaven with the angels.

Your Majesty: Robbie

I have to tell you about Mrs. Salter, or should I say Your Majesty. Several years ago, Mom and Dad kept telling me they wanted me to visit Mrs. Salter at her house. I didn't know why they wanted me to go to her house when I could see Mrs. Salter at work. Anyway, one day after work, Mom made plans for us to stop by her house. When we got there, Mrs. Salter let us in and said that she heard I loved Disney. She then took me around her house, where she has glass cases of every Disney character.

As soon as I would say "Well, I don't see Ariel," she would take me around the corner, and there would be another case with more Disney characters. I couldn't believe it. It was like being in a Disney castle. And I was. I was in a castle, and Mrs. Salter was the queen with everything Disney. So I now call her Your Majesty. Your Majesty was so nice to let me in her house and share with me her love of Disney too. We talked about all the different characters, which ones were her favorites, and which were mine. She said I could come back anytime. I love Your Majesty.

Disney Jeopardy: Robbie

I have always loved Disney movies since I was very little. Some of the very first Disney movies I remember watching are *Beauty and the Beast* and *Aladdin*. I loved all the characters, music, backgrounds, and just how magical they were. When I was twelve years old, I was on my computer when I realized I could find out who the voices of all the Disney characters were. I was so excited and started learning as much as I could about all the Disney movies.

I started to learn not only which actors/actresses did voices of which characters but also who drew all the animations for the characters, which brought them to life. Then there was all the editing, music, writing, sound production, directing, etc.

I was able to learn not only all this about each of the Disney movies but also what year they were released and then if they were ever nominated for any awards. Like *Snow White and the Seven Dwarfs*, 1937, is the first full-animated feature film in motion picture history. *Fantasia* is the first animated film shown in stereophonic sound. *Song of the South* is first film that used live actors, who provided a sentimental frame story for several animated segments. *Cinderella* was Disney's most successful film since *Snow White and the Seven Dwarfs*. *Treasure Island* is the first all-live-action feature film.

Lady and the Tramp is first animated film in CinemaScope. *Sleeping Beauty* is first animated film in Super Technirama 70mm. The film 101 Dalmatians is the first animated feature film to use Xerox cels. *Mary Poppins* is the most successful Disney film ever. *Beauty and the Beast* is the first animated film nominated for an Academy Award for

Best Picture. *The Lion King* became the highest-grossing traditionally animated film in history. *Toy Story* is the first computer-animated feature film produced by Pixar.

Chicken Little is the first fully computer-animated film. *Up* is first computer-animated film and second animated film nominated for an Academy Award for Best Picture. *Frozen* became the highest-grossing computer animated film in history. I will never forget anything about Disney.I could go on and on about all the Disney things I know. So maybe my next book will be all about Disney movies.

But I will save for that another day. I will not forget.

Meeting a Legend: Robbie

My mom told me the legendary autistic woman Temple Grandin was coming to Birmingham, Alabama, and asked if I wanted to go see her. I knew who Temple was since I watched a movie about her, *Temple Grandin*. It was a really good movie, which was all about Temple's life. My mom and I watched her movie together. At the end of it, my mom was upset 'cause I was crying. I told her I was crying because I finally understood and now I knew there were other people just like me.

Mom, Emma, and I headed to Birmingham to listen to Temple speak. When we first got there, Mom went to save seats up front for us. Once we had our seats saved, Mom had to go to the bathroom. Emma and I were standing outside waiting for her when Emma and I saw Temple Grandin walk toward us. She saw us standing there with all her books and the movie in our hands. She said, "I will sign those, but I have go to the restroom first."

My mom came back out, and Emma and I were like, "Did you just see her? Temple just went in there with you. Did you not see her? She's in there right now! She is going to come back out and sign our books. We just talked to her."

A few minutes later, Temple came out of the bathroom and signed her name on all our books and her DVD movie. Temple also took a picture with me.

Temple then asked me, "Do you have a job?" I said, "Yes, I have worked for the Ledges since I was sixteen!" She said, "Good!" I was so excited to meet her and had never met a celebrity before. I wanted to tell her how much we were alike and how I was writing a book about my life, just like she did. But she didn't want to hear anything about that; she just wanted to know if I had a job.

It was time for her presentation to start. We had good seats and got to listen to her speak about experiences she has had in life. She said it was very important that autistic kids stay involved. That they should get jobs as soon as possible. She did not like that some of the kids there were playing on their iPads or phones. In fact, she took one girl's iPad away and another boy's phone away. She said it was important that they learn to interact and listen to people.

She told us about how her mom always made her fit in and keep up with everyone. Temple is right. If I wanted to, I could have just sat back and not say anything to anyone and not raise my hand in class or anything. But I want to hang out with other kids. I want to be involved. I like having time to myself, but it get lonely being by myself all the time. I love it when I get to see my friends and be around other people.

Getting to meet Temple was a day I will never forget. She has shown me that I can be or do anything I want to. I really appreciate that she took time to sign our books and take pictures with us.

All-Star Employee: Dad

Finding a person with autism who can work in any capacity is worth its weight in gold. I recommend to anyone looking for hiring the most loyal employee you will ever have to consider by reaching out to your local autism resource and finding someone who meets your needs. They will be all over the spectrum in terms of ability, but find one that matches, and it will be a great experience for your fellow employees and the family of the person with autism. That is a big fear of all parents of children with autism. Will they be a productive adult?

We are very fortunate in that respect. Robbie has worked for me since he was sixteen years old. He is now getting ready to turn twenty-three and has never missed a day of work, never been late for work, and never complained at work. That doesn't mean he doesn't sometimes struggle in his position whenever something doesn't go as planned, but it has taught him that it's okay to not be perfect.

He sometimes has difficulty with the bending of rules when it applies to our business, but he has become much better at letting it go and just rolling with the flow. He started as a golf club cleaner and did it better than anyone has done it in my twenty-seven years of the business. He has graduated to running the parking lot, greeting golfers, and running golf events. He doesn't miss a beat. I'm very proud of him at work, and it's great to see him blossom into this great employee and fine man.

Meet Ali: Robbie

Mom worked at Barnes & Noble for over ten years. One day, she came home from work and told me that she needed my help. She would, every once in a while, come home and tell me that she would need Emma and me to help her with work. However, this time, it was a surprise Mom had for me. It was Ali MacGraw! She was coming to Huntsville, and Mom wanted me to help her with the autograph signing. Mom was going to get the book that *Love Story* was made from and the DVD and Blu-ray for her to sign. I couldn't believe this. I was so excited. Ali MacGraw was nominated for an Academy Award for Best Actress.

On the day of the event, my mom and I set the table up with all the books and movies. Everyone wanted to buy the book and movie and was excited to have her sign them. Ali came in and sat at a small stage, where the director of the Huntsville Art Museum talked to her and asked her all kinds of questions about her life and career. She was very funny, and everyone just loved her. After she finished speaking to everyone, she began signing all the books and movies. She took pictures with everyone and was so nice.

Some people stood in line for over an hour just to meet her. Mom and I were really lucky because our table was next to her, so we were by her all night long. She took pictures, signed books, and talked to everyone for almost three hours before it was getting really late. I still could not believe that Ali MacGraw was sitting in a chair right next to me.

It was really late, and Ali was tired from a long day of meeting people. But Mom and I got at the end of the line, hoping that she wouldn't mind signing our books and movies before leaving. We knew how tired she was, and everyone was ready to go home. She was so nice to us. Not only did she sign our stuff, but she also took a couple of pictures with us and asked me what my name was. She wanted to thank me for coming out and helping. She was also scheduled to do another lunch event the next day and thought she would be seeing us again. However, I had to work the next day and wasn't able to go help my mom again.

The next morning, when my mom got to the event and they finished up and Ali was done meeting everyone, my mom thanked her again for being so nice to us and taking time to meet us last night. Ali asked her where I was. My mom told her I had to work and how much I loved getting to meet her. Ali told my mom she just loved me and really appreciated me coming out and helping last night. I will never forget Ali MacGraw and how nice she was to me. I only hope that I will get to meet her again one day.

Life Goes On: Emma

Probably one of the hardest moments in my life was saying good-bye to my brother when I left for college. People don't understand how amazing my brother is. He sees the absolute best in everything. Our rooms are connected at home, and knowing I wouldn't just be able to sit and listen to him jump up and down just saddened me. He also could hear when I was upset and would come into my room and always put a smile on my face, and knowing I wouldn't see that bright smile hurt me.

I think the hardest part of it was the fact of leaving him; he would now be all alone. Once Robbie graduated, he never got to see his friends anymore. He had work and other little things, but he never really got the socialization from school. It was Robbie and me at home just lying around. We wouldn't talk all the time, but we would watch Disney movies and just sit there together. He doesn't need someone to talk to as much as you would think. It's just nice to know someone is there as I won't be there anymore.

When he and my parents left after moving me in, I didn't want to let him go. I cried and cried and cried some more. There were days when I just wished I could see his big smile and have one of his bear hugs, but I remembered this is life, and we both had plans ahead of us.

New Home: Robbie

One day, my mom and dad got an e-mail from Hayley Henderson, whom I know from the Ledges, where I work. Hayley asked my parents about having me go to classes at Merrimack Hall. Merrimack Hall is a performing arts center. I was not sure about that because I am not a performer, dancer, or singer. Those are not my things, and I really don't have an interest in them.

Anyway, before I could go to any of the classes, I had to go and meet with Rachel. Rachel was in charge of the classes and asked me a bunch of questions. Rachel told us that she thought I would be a good fit for their connection class. In this class, they do all kinds of things, and art was one of them. I'm an artist, so I accepted, but I was not going to do the singing and dancing part. I am okay listing to the Disney songs, which I know all of them, but I never dream about singing because I am not a singer. My dad fixed my schedule at work so that I could go to the connection class on Thursday mornings.

I remember the first day my mom took me to the connection class and dropped me off. Rachel introduced me to everyone, who were all so nice. I got to meet Debra Jenkins and her daughter Emma, who were excited to meet me. Hayley also came by and checked on me to make sure I was doing fine. Whenever it would be singing time, I just watched everyone as I am not a singer. But when it was art time, I got to draw. A bunch of people would just watch me and tell me how good my drawing was. They would say, "You're an artist."

I have made so many new friends at Merrimack. I loved getting to go not only on Thursdays to Connection but now to a writing class on

Mondays. It was so nice to get to see my new friends every week. I did participate in the last performance they had as the grumpy bus driver, but I don't want to do that again. I'm not a performer, and it's not my thing. But I can help make sure everyone else knows what and where he or she is suppose to be. I am good at following directions.

My Happy Son: Mom

Everyone knows of Robbie as the happy kid. The baby that had the cutest smile and contagious laugh and loved big hugs. But as his mom, I ask, is he really always happy? He has his moments, just like we all do, but does he seem happier than the average person? Yes. This is so hard at times. How can he be this happy when he has never experienced spending the night with a friend, going on a date, having his phone ring with calls from friends or *the* girl, getting his driver's license, and going to homecoming, prom, or college?

My heart breaks even as I type this, thinking that Robbie may grow old with only me, his dad, and Emma. I feel bad when I come home from work on a day when he has been home alone all day and when I don't spend some time with him, real-time interacting. Just having someone to watch a show with, someone to hear about what he's learned for the day, someone to be there when he has that one thing to say. Yes, I do think he enjoys his time alone, but just how much? Day after day of being by yourself, is that really being happy?

If you've been a regular to our house, then you have probably heard Robbie in his room having a good ole time, but with whom? His friends? Yes, while Robbie is home days on end by himself, he has his "friends" that will play and act out over and over with him a Disney video from YouTube or play trivia with him. These friends are just like the characters in the movie *Inside Out*. Yep, Robbie has his own Joy and Sadness that live inside him.

He always says he's good and fine by himself, but as his mom, I don't want him to be by himself, and as his mom, I know differently. I know he is lonely. I know he really wants friends to be with. I want him to have friends—friends that he hangs out with and talks to on a regular basis. I am terrified of the day that I will no longer be here for him. Yes, Robbie can fix his own food, shower, and take care of himself. I don't have to remind Robbie to open doors for others, to say "Thank you," or to wait patiently for his turn.

All these lessons he has learned, and trust me, once an autistic individual learns something, they never forget it. But he is alone. I want what other parents want for their children: to one day find the love of their life, get married, and have a family. I do so want this for him, but will it ever happen? I know that Emma will never let Robbie be alone, but even with him being a part of her life, that is not what we all dream of for our kids.

That is such a heavy responsibility to put on Emma. Emma needs to and should be like other college students and plan for her own future, which is enough to bear these days. But Emma carries the responsibility with her of "If I choose this, will that work for me and Robbie?" or "If I do this, then that might be better for me and Robbie."

I know that I have robbed Emma so much of her own childhood. I can remember back as young as her being almost three and Robbie being five and telling her to hold his hand and not let go. Not to mention every time Emma and Robbie would go somewhere, I would drill her with one hundred questions, Emma having to answer for the both of them. Wow, this was so wrong of me. And as Emma got older, she became the mom to a volleyball team because this was simply all she knew.

So why is it so easy for Robbie to be happy? Because he feels loved. Because God has blessed him with an unbelievable gift, a gift to make others feel good and loved even when he himself may be lonely or sad. Robbie strives to please others. If he gets mad about something or says something upsetting, it's only minutes before he comes looking for a hug with a big "I'm sorry." Robbie does what we want of him—to be happy.

The Whys: Robbie

When I was little, I didn't like to eat any food that wasn't room temperature. Why? I really don't know. It burned my mouth if it was too cold and hurt if it was too hot. I also remember while I was in school, I always had fried chicken, a bag of plain chips, Jell-O, and two cookies with a juice for lunch every day. Everyone would always ask, "Don't you get tired of having the same thing? But I didn't.

When I got to high school, I started eating lunch at school. They would always have different things. So I guess this might be when I started eating different things. I also always used to want hamburger on Sundays. But now I will eat just about anything. I love steak, crawfish, spaghetti, lasagna, broccoli, and potatoes, and one of my favorites is Caesar salad. Some things that I just didn't like when I was little, I like now. Why? I don't really know, but my mom would tell me it's good for my heart, so I would try them.

When I was little, I wanted so bad to go to the theater to see the new Disney movies coming out, but it would hurt my ears; it was so loud. My mom would give me these things to put in my ears to try and help with the sound, but it just made the sounds echo even louder. Emma would get upset 'cause we couldn't go to the movies as a family.

Once again, when I was a little older, we went back to the theatre, and I was okay. I love going to the movies now. They are loud and sometimes still hurt my ears a little, but it's okay. Why doesn't it hurt my ears anymore? I don't know. Maybe, I am just able to handle it better. I don't really know, but it's okay, and I love the movies.

I used to only want to go see Disney and Pixar movies, and they had to be animation. Why? I don't know. Maybe it is 'cause that is what I liked. It was what I knew and understood. But now I enjoy all kinds of movies. I like seeing the movies that are up for awards, but Disney movies are still my favorite.

Same thing with TV. When I was little, I would only watch Disney, Cartoon Network, or Nickelodeon shows. Today, I still love Disney but also love watching all kinds of things. I love the Game Show channel, and of course, the *Amazing Race* is one of my favorites.

So what I am trying to say is, I don't always know why. Just because someone doesn't like or just won't do something when they are little doesn't mean they won't grow out of it and try it later. I used to not like any kind of change at all, but I am okay with it. Now I do get upset when I get my schedule for work and I'm off on certain days, but then they go back and change it where I have to work. This upsets me, but it's okay. I understand that, sometimes, things just have to change. It's no one's fault. It just happens.

The Hardest Thing: Dad

Relative to autism, I only have one thing that I am scared of. I am sure it is the same with all parents of special needs children. What's going to happen to my child when I am no longer here to care for him? That is my biggest fear. That is what drives me, and it is what drives our decisions based on our family. The day I leave this earth, I want to make sure Robbie is financially set, where if he couldn't find a job, he would be able to live comfortably for the rest of his life.

My fears go way beyond this, though. Who will take care of him to make sure he is safe, healthy, and not taken advantage of? Who will be responsible for paying his bills and getting him to and from a job and to and from a doctor? Should this be the responsibility of his sister? It's not fair to put that responsibility on her and her family. My daughter will be the first to sign up for that job, and I am so proud of her, but I'm not sure if it's the best decision for either of them.

We all want our children to be happy, healthy, and successful. We also want them to have someone to share their life with—a partner to help look after each other, to share the day with, someone one can depend on. Will Robbie ever have this? Will Robbie ever have that someone special to share his life with?

What's Next: Robbie

For the past four years, I've been telling everyone about my book. Now what? What do I do now? My mom always told me, "You either go to school or go to work." Well, I don't care to go to school anymore, and I already go to work. If I didn't work at the Ledges, I would miss all the people there that have been so nice to me. I also don't want to have to learn something else, so the Ledges is a good place for me.

My mom also showed me where some people have already asked if I would come tell my story to some teachers and sign my book. I guess like what Temple does when we went to see her in Birmingham. I think I can do that. I am nervous. I hope everyone will be able to understand me and what I am trying to say. I also hope I will be able to understand what they are asking me.

I know everyone has to grow up, but sometimes it is hard being me and figuring out things in my life. But I know it's not just me—that you guys also have trouble figuring things out too. What is your dream about your life? And what are your feelings about yourself? Try to think about your life and understand what it's about and how your life fits in with the rest of the world. That's what I do. And last, always be positive and try not to give up.

I would like to thank all my family and friends:
All the teachers and staff of the Baton Rouge
Speech and Hearing Foundation
Teachers and staff of Westminster Elementary School
Teachers and staff of Challenger Elementary School
Teachers and staff of Challenger Middle School
Teachers and staff of Grissom High School

Doctors and therapists:
Aunt, Dr. Sharon Lee Barksdale
Dr. Greg Gelpi
Sheran Samuel Benton
Jenni Santoura
Dr. Stephanie Cave
Dr. Ann Chu

Note: A percent of the proceeds from my
book sales will go back to benefit
Merrimack Hall.
Thank you to Merrimack Hall for giving me a new place to call home.

CPSIA information can be obtained
at www.ICGtesting.com
Printed in the USA
FSHW011343090920
73651FS